A Literature Unit for

The Red Pony

by John Steinbeck

Written by Mari Lu Robbins

Illustrated by Cheryl Buhler

Teacher Created Materials
P.O. Box 1040
Huntington Beach, CA 92647
© *1994 Teacher Created Materials, Inc.*
Made in U.S.A.
ISBN 1-55734-443-4

The classroom teacher may reproduce copies of materials in this book for classroom use only. The reproduction of any part for an entire school or school system is strictly prohibited. No part of this publication may be transmitted, stored, or recorded in any form without written permission from the publisher.

Table of Contents

Introduction 3
Sample Lesson Plans 4
Before the Book *(Pre-reading Activities)* 5
About the Author 6
Book Summary 7
Vocabulary Lists 8
Vocabulary Activities 9
SECTION 1 *(First half of "The Gift")* 10
- ❖ Quiz Time!
- ❖ Hands-On Project—*Knotting*
- ❖ Cooperative Learning Activity—*Anticipation Guide*
- ❖ Curriculum Connections—Meteorology: *Cloud Formations*
- ❖ Into Your Life—*Reading Response Journals*

SECTION 2 *(Second half of "The Gift")* 15
- ❖ Quiz Time!
- ❖ Hands-On Project—*Make a Hair Hygrometer*
- ❖ Cooperative Activity—*Scientific Scavenger Hunt*
- ❖ Curriculum Connections—Science: *Antibiotics*
- ❖ Into Your Life—*A New Kind of Pioneer*

SECTION 3 *("The Great Mountains")* 20
- ❖ Quiz Time!
- ❖ Hands-On Activity—*Making a Piñata*
- ❖ Cooperative Activity—*Can You Hear Feelings?*
- ❖ Curriculum Connections—History: *California's Hispanic Legacy*
- ❖ Into Your Life—*Nonverbal Signs of Listening*

SECTION 4 *("The Promise")* 25
- ❖ Quiz Time!
- ❖ Hands-On Activity—*Tempting Tapioca*
- ❖ Cooperative Activity—*Honoring the Nobel Winners*
- ❖ Curriculum Connections—Geography: *The Salinas Valley*
- ❖ Into Your Life—*Present a Literary Award*

SECTION 5 *("The Leader of the People")* 30
- ❖ Quiz Time!
- ❖ Hands-On Activity—*Build a Covered Wagon*
- ❖ Cooperative Activity—*Build a Corral*
- ❖ Curriculum Connection—Language Arts: *Descriptive Writing*
- ❖ Into Your Life—*Become a Book Illustrator!*

After the Book *(Post-reading Activities)*

   Any Questions? 35
   Book Report Ideas 36
   Research Ideas 37
Culminating Activity 38
Unit Test Options 41
Sample Response Journal Questions 44
Bibliography of Related Reading 45
Answer Key 46

Introduction

Nothing can quite match the power and joy a good book can bring to our lives. In a superb book such as *The Red Pony*, we encounter characters who inspire and comfort us with their courage, and words that impress us with their beauty and artistry. Furthermore, we can return to such a book over and over, finding new pleasures each time.

In *Literature Units* we have taken great care to select books of quality to which one can return for enjoyment over the years.

This unit contains the following features to supplement the teacher's own valuable ideas and inspirations.

- Sample Lesson Plans

- Pre-reading Activities

- Biographical Sketch and Picture of the Author

- Book Summary

- Vocabulary Lists and Suggested Vocabulary Ideas

- Chapters grouped for study with each section including a (an):

    — *quiz*

    — *hands-on project*

    — *cooperative learning activity*

    — *cross-curricular connection*

    — *extension into the reader's life*

- Post-reading Activities

- Book Report Ideas

- Research Ideas

- Culminating Activities

- Three Different Options for Unit Tests

- Bibliography

- Answer Key

We are confident this unit will be a valuable addition to your planning, and we hope that as you use our ideas, your students will increase the circle of "friends" they have in books!

The Red Pony

Sample Lesson Plan

Each of the lessons suggested below can take from one to several days to complete.

Lesson 1
- Introduce and complete some or all of the pre-reading activities found on page 5.
- Read "About the Author" with your students (page 6).
- Read the book summary with your students (page 7).
- Introduce the vocabulary list for Section 1 (page 8).

Lesson 2
- Read first half of "The Gift." As you read, place the vocabulary words in the context of the story and discuss their meanings.
- Do a vocabulary activity (page 9).
- Learn to knot (page 11).
- Complete an anticipation guide (page 12).
- Discuss the book in terms of cloud formations and how they may have affected the story of "The Gift" (page 13).
- Begin "Reading Response Journals" (page 14).
- Administer the Section 1 Quiz (page 10).
- Introduce vocabulary list for Section 2 (page 8).

Lesson 3
- Read second half of "The Gift." Place the vocabulary words in context and discuss their meanings.
- Do a vocabulary activity (page 9).
- Make a hair hygrometer (page 16).
- Go on a scientific scavenger hunt (page 17).
- Learn about the discovery of antibiotics and discuss how their availability might have changed the story of "The Gift" (page 18).
- Become a new pioneer by taking a survey about modern changes in medicine (page 19).
- Administer the Section 2 Quiz (page 15).
- Introduce the vocabulary words for Section 3 (page 8).

Lesson 4
- Read "The Great Mountains." Place the vocabulary words in context and discuss their meanings.
- Do a vocabulary activity (page 9).
- Make a piñata (page 21).
- Learn the importance of really hearing what other people are saying (page 22).
- Learn about California's Hispanic legacy and its possible influence on Gitano (page 23).
- Practice ways to listen better (page 24).
- Administer the Section 3 quiz (page 20).
- Introduce the vocabulary list for Section 4 (page 8).

Lesson 5
- Read "The Promise." Place the vocabulary words in context and discuss their meanings.
- Do a vocabulary activity (page 9).
- Make tapioca pudding (page 26).
- Research a Nobel Prize in Literature winner (page 27).
- Learn about the Salinas Valley (page 28).
- Nominate your favorite author for a literary award (page 29).
- Administer the Section 4 quiz (page 25).
- Introduce the vocabulary words for Section 5 (page 8).

Lesson 6
- Read "The Leader of the People." Place the vocabulary words in context and discuss their meanings.
- Do a vocabulary activity (page 9).
- Create a model covered wagon (page 31).
- Construct a model corral of covered wagons (page 32).
- Learn how to write a good descriptive paragraph (page 33).
- Illustrate a scene from *The Red Pony* (page 34).
- Administer the Section 5 quiz (page 30).

Lesson 7
- Discuss any questions your students may have about the story (page 35).
- Assign book report and research projects (pages 36 and 37).
- Begin work on culminating activity (pages 38, 39, and 40).

Lesson 8
- Administer unit test 1, 2, and/or 3 (pages 41 to 43).
- Discuss test answers and responses.
- Discuss students' opinions and enjoyment of the book.
- Provide a list of related reading for the students (page 45).

Lesson 9
- Celebrate with the Old West culminating activity (pages 38-40).

Pre-Reading Activities   *The Red Pony*

Before the Book

Before they begin *The Red Pony*, your students will benefit from gaining a feel for the time period of the story as well as the cultural framework in which it is set. Some prior knowledge of the book's setting and other relevant information will enable them to better understand the importance of events in the story and to relate to the story's characters. Learning to anticipate what is going to happen in the story will help them focus on events and motivation, thereby increasing their comprehension. Here are some activities that may work for you.

1. Predict what the story might be about by hearing the title.

2. Predict what the story might be about by looking at the cover.

3. Discuss other books by John Steinbeck that students may have read previously. What kinds of backgrounds do many of his stories and books have?

4. Discuss the "Westward Movement" in 19th century America.

5. Discuss "western" movies and television shows the students may have watched and their characteristics. How was life portrayed in them? Do the movies and television show life as it really was, or might some aspects of western life have been exaggerated or distorted? If so, why might they have been?

6. What would a child's life have been like on a farm in the days before radio, television, VCR's, and computer games?

7. Complete the Anticipation Guide (page 12) and discuss some of the answers. Save these until the book has been read and discuss the same questions with the students again to determine what, if any, changes have occurred in their opinions as a result of reading the book.

8. Ask the students whether a person or a pet they loved has ever died. Discuss how it feels to suffer the loss of a beloved person or pet. Talk about the grieving process and how it might affect individual people differently.

9. Write descriptions of what grief is. What color is it? How long does it last? How can you tell when it is over? What might happen if one did not allow himself/herself to grieve?

10. Do people always show their true feelings?

About the Author

John Steinbeck was born February 27, 1902, in Salinas, California. The Salinas Valley and nearby Monterey County provide the settings for many of his books and stories. He grew up in Salinas in the Victorian house where he was born. This house still stands near the downtown area and is now a luncheon restaurant. His grandparents, Samuel and Elizabeth Hamilton, had a ranch south of Salinas near King City, and in summers he often was taken by his uncle, Tom Hamilton, to visit the ranch before it was sold in 1912. Steinbeck graduated from Salinas High School in 1919 and spent several years at Stanford University before leaving to pursue a full-time writing career in New York.

Steinbeck began writing at a very early age. His boyhood friend, William Black, remembered Steinbeck at the age of fourteen or fifteen showing him "at least" fifty completed manuscripts, handwritten on white paper, all about the Salinas Valley. Mr. Black said that the stories were exciting and that one of them was a short story about a pony. Steinbeck did, in fact, have a beloved pony of his own, and pictures exist of him and his sister, Mary, together on the pony.

John Steinbeck wrote many books, publishing twenty-nine. The most famous of these probably were *The Red Pony, The Grapes of Wrath, The Pearl, Tortilla Flat, The Winter of Our Discontent,* and *Cannery Row*. He was the recipient of many awards, including the Pulitzer Prize Fiction Award, the Nobel Prize for Literature, and the United States Medal of Freedom.

A master of description, Steinbeck could turn an ordinary event into something extraordinary. In *The Red Pony*, for example, the first appearance of Gitano involves a sequence of powerful details describing the mysterious old man. Finally, he becomes an emblem of durability and dignity, a tribute to the land, the past, and the people of California.

Steinbeck shunned publicity and lived for many years before his death in secluded Sag Harbor on Long Island, New York. He died December 20, 1968, in New York, and his ashes are buried in Salinas, the city of his birth.

Book Summary

The Red Pony

by John Steinbeck

(USA, Viking Child Books; Canada, Penguin; UK & AUS, Penguin Ltd.)

The Red Pony is not strictly a novel in the usual sense but is instead a masterpiece of four interrelated stories which center on the experiences of a little boy growing up on a ranch in California's Salinas Valley during the early 1900's.

In the first story, "The Gift," the little boy, Jody, is given a pony by his father. For months Jody hopes, plans, and dreams of the day when he will finally be able to ride this beautiful animal, which he names Gabilan after the nearby mountains. His best friend on the ranch, Billy Buck the cowhand, teaches Jody all the many things he must learn to become a good horseman.

The second story, "The Great Mountains," is almost an allegory, a story in which characters take on symbolic meanings. An old man, Gitano, walks to the ranch and announces, "I have come back," back to the place where he was born. Gitano stays for a few days, largely against the wishes of Jody's father, Carl, who thinks the old man is too old to be useful on the ranch. Gitano sees a parallel between himself and Carl's old horse, Easter, and one day he and Easter disappear together, headed for the mountains.

In "The Promise," Jody once again has hope of someday riding his own horse. His father gives him a chance to earn the colt which their mare, Nellie, will be dropping after eleven months. As Nellie's time approaches, however, Jody remembers the grief of losing his first pony. Billy Buck assures him that everything will be all right but is aware that in the back of Jody's mind there is doubt because Billy was wrong before. Finally, the colt arrives at a high and unexpected cost as Billy tries to regain his former stature in Jody's eyes.

In the last story of the quartet, "The Leader of the People," Jody and his grandfather experience a loving, mutually supportive relationship. Grandfather had been the leader of a wagon train crossing the mountains to California, and Jody idolizes him. Jody has never been away from his small community, and he yearns to go across the mountains to "see what he could see," as his mother puts it. The most exciting thing in Jody's own life at this time is a mouse hunt, and to him his grandfather is bigger than life, a fearless man who came from a race of giants. Jody wants to lead the people west like his grandfather, but when his grandfather explains that the westering movement has finished, Jody makes Grandfather a glass of lemonade, knowing that his own opportunities to flourish someday will come.

The Red Pony

Vocabulary Lists

On this page are vocabulary lists which correspond to each sectional grouping of *The Red Pony* as outlined in the table of contents (page 2). Ideas for activities using these words can be found on page 9 of this book.

John Steinbeck was a master of the English language, and placing a significant focus on the study of the words he used is well worthwhile.

Section 1

emerge	protrude	chambray	corral	frenzied
muskmelon	muffled	reservations	lowing	dignity
bandy-legged	curry	oilcloth	lax	girded
quartz	carrion	hampered	irritably	disparaging
contemplative	vicinity	doom	incipient	scalded
fatigue	hackamore	induced	hackles	coax

Section 2

pommel	putrify	writhe	reproachful	contempt
solemn	listless	grope	convulsive	volunteer (grass)
rambunctious	nicker	geometric	fallible	coddling
precede	mope	luster	whetted	provocative
shamble	taut	hedged	obstruction	flanks
constricted	withers	ague	carborundum	incensed

Section 3

impulse	perspective	ferocious	aloof	clodhopper
gnarled	colander	repose	parallel	relent
agony	disemboweled	despair	contrast	trudge
confront	paisano	inflexible	diffident	hame-bells
strenuous	potential	imperturbability	impersonal	abrupt
rebuke	rapier	hilt	smolder	intricate

Section 4

bewildered	clabber	construed	unprecedented	metallic
scabbard	docile	peonage	dam	languorous
axis	nonchalance	shrivel	paternal	complacent
many-tined	frantic	geld	counteract	restive
strident	desolation	perpetual	epaulet	spasm
dappled	conjunction	preliminary	trilling	martial

Section 5

burrow	elaborate	entangle	rancor	boast
tonal	regret	staunch	flail	philosophical
ominous	judicious	interlace	plod	humoring
draft cattle	dirge	piteous	apprehension	westering
earnest	translate	cleft	reverence	immune
kerosene	frontier	explanatory	retract	disconsolate

#443 Literature Unit | 8 | © 1994 Teacher Created Materials, Inc.

The Red Pony

Vocabulary Activities

These vocabulary activities are ones which may be used at your discretion for the vocabulary words in each section of *The Red Pony*. Some of the words have been used in a different way than your students may have expected to see them, and the activities should be completed using the meanings in the book. Using the words outside the context of the book will help your students to better understand the full meaning of the book itself. Combine these activites with your own valuable ideas to further enrich your students' vocabularies.

- **Build a dictionary:** To aid your students' use of alphabetizing, as well as learning new meanings, compile a class dictionary on chart paper or in a composition book. As words are added to the dictionary, record and discuss alternative meanings to help students get an understanding of the great complexity and flexibility of the English language.

- **Poll taking:** As a homework assignment, have the students ask friends and relatives what they think are the meanings of selected words. Students then record all answers which are given and bring them to class. Guesses are accepted! This is a fun assignment, and students will enjoy sharing the "meanings" they have collected.

- **Match words to definitions:** Put words in one column and meanings in another. Have students match meanings to words.

- **Synonyms:** Present sentences in which the underlined synonym of a vocabulary word is used. Students choose which of three or four vocabulary words best expresses the meaning of the underlined word.

- **Word form:** Provide the root form of the vocabulary word in parentheses after a sentence in which a blank needs to be filled by the correct form of the word. For example, "Daydreaming in the sun, the_____ boy forgot his homework." (Languor)

- **Play Jeopardy:** On the board, list meanings of the words under category headings. When called on, the student chooses a category and "level" and must then tell which word fits the meaning chosen. If the answer is correct, the student earns a point; if the answer is not correct, another student may try to answer for the point instead. This may be played as a team game if you wish, and the students try to earn points for their teams.

- **"Fractured Words":** In groups, students write a paragraph in which words sounding similar to a given number of vocabulary words, but which have different meanings, are substituted for the correct words. The group then presents its paragraph to the class to see whether the other students can detect which words are used incorrectly and supply the correct words. For example: "John wants to *detract* his first answer." (for *retract*)

Section 1: First half of "The Gift" *The Red Pony*

Quiz Time!

1. On the back of this paper, list three important events in Section 1.

2. Describe Jody's home where this story takes place.
   _____
   _____
   _____

3. Who is Billy Buck?
   _____
   _____

4. What kind of father is Carl Tiflin?
   _____
   _____

5. What is the surprise Carl Tiflin and Billy Buck have for Jody?
   _____
   _____

6. What does Jody have to wait for, and why does he have to wait?
   _____
   _____

7. How do the kids at school react when Jody tells them of his surprise?
   _____
   _____

8. What does Billy Buck teach Jody?
   _____
   _____

9. What does Billy Buck have Jody collect, and why does he have him collect it?
   _____
   _____

10. Why does Carl Tiflin object to the way Jody trained Gabilan?
    _____
    _____
    _____

#443 Literature Unit © 1994 Teacher Created Materials, Inc.

Section 1: First half of "The Gift" *The Red Pony*

Knotting

Billy Buck makes a hair rope for Jody to use on Gabilan. While using horse tail hair to make a rope may seem strange to us, it actually was a very common practice in the days when many people lived on ranches or farms. Horse hair was available; it was free; and it was very strong.

Since before written history, people have made rope from many different materials: vines, reeds, leather and, after people began growing it, cotton. Many ropes today are made from synthetic materials such as nylon. On a ranch, rope may be used for bridles and halters, lifting heavy objects, pulling, and securing, among other uses. Many different kinds of knots have been invented for various purposes by ranchers, sailors, fishermen, prospectors, packers, and surgeons.

Several kinds of knots are illustrated below. Try your hand at making some of these knots. Do you know any others? It has been said that only three new knots have been invented since 1900. Can you come up with one which you do not see illustrated here? You will need a short length of rope or cord and perhaps a dowel or stick for some knots.

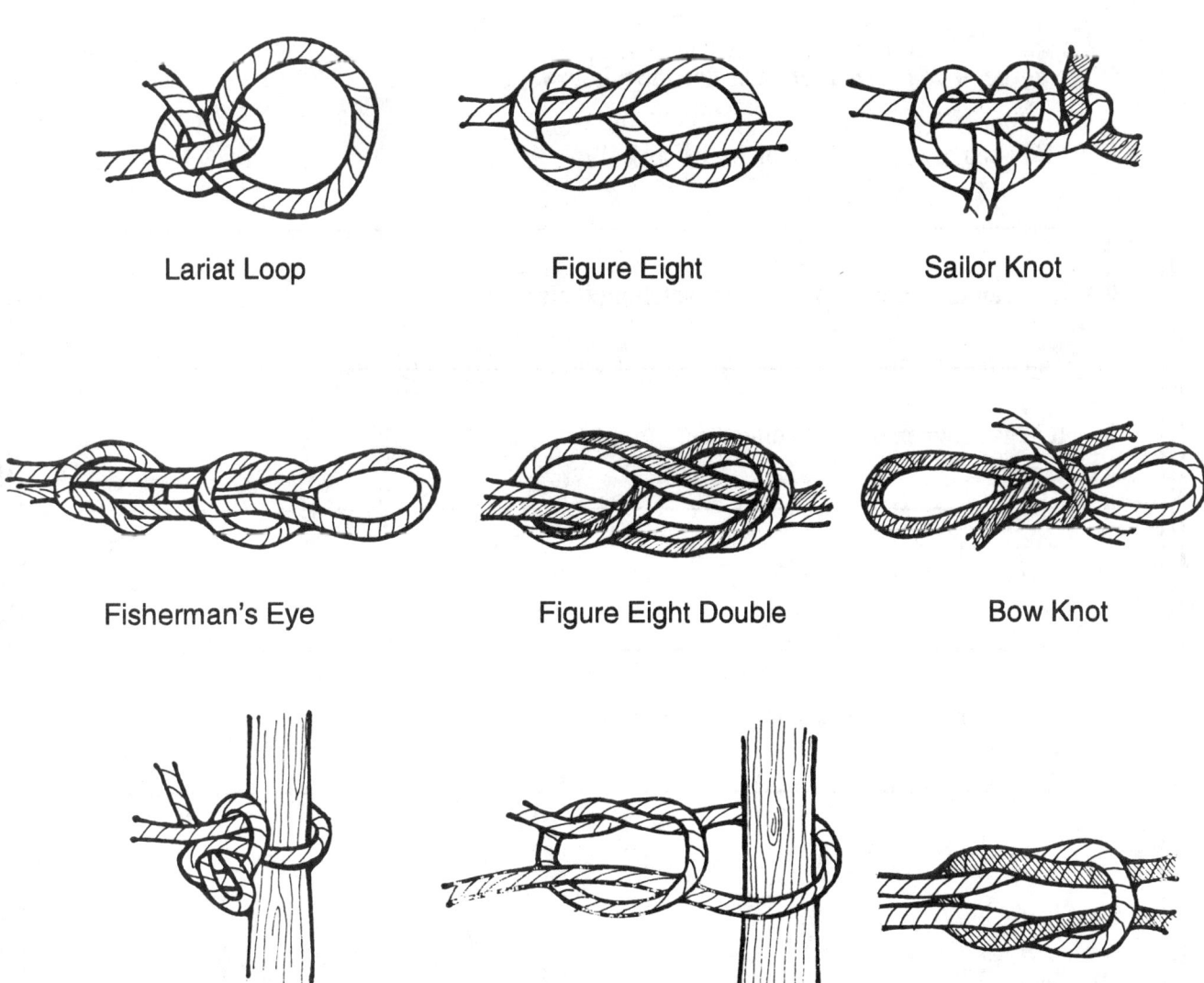

Section 1: First half of "The Gift" *The Red Pony*

Anticipation Guide

Use this anticipation guide to set a tone for reading *The Red Pony* and to bring to mind familiar situations that will help students relate both conceptually and emotionally with the story.

Before you begin the book, show its cover to the class and tell them they will be reading *The Red Pony*. In groups of three or four, fill out the anticipation guide. Emphasize to the students that their answers are opinions only and will not be graded. Collect papers when they are completed.

After collecting the anticipation guides and without disclosing identities, discuss the answers with the entire class. When they have finished reading the book, repeat filling out the guides, and discuss any changes of opinion between the first and second papers.

Anticipation Guide

Write *agree* or *disagree* after each statement below.

1. "You can always tell a book by its cover."
   _____

2. You can tell how people feel by watching their faces.
   _____

3. It is good when dreams come true.
   _____

4. No one wants to die.
   _____

5. Death, while sometimes hard to understand, is a part of life.
   _____

Section 1: First Half of "The Gift" *The Red Pony*

Cloud Formations

Meteorologists are scientists who forecast the weather and measure rainfall. During the time of *The Red Pony*, weather forecasting and measurement of rainfall, air pressure, and the huge bodies of air masses called fronts, were attempted but without the benefit of computers and weather satellites which meteorologists now use. When Billy Buck wanted to predict the weather, he had to rely on his own interpretations of natural signs, such as cloud patterns as seen from the ground, hair on caterpillars, bird migration, and hibernation of animals.

We now know how clouds form in the atmosphere and what each kind of cloud formation means. There are three main kinds of clouds, and they form at different heights in the air. Wispy **cirrus** clouds are the highest clouds. Lower than cirrus clouds are different kinds of **cumulus** clouds, the large, fluffy, white clouds which appear so pretty to us. One kind of cumulus cloud is the **cumulonimbus** storm cloud. This kind of cloud, which sometimes is said to have an "anvil shape" because it is shaped like a blacksmith's anvil, is a typical thunderstorm cloud. Airplane pilots try to avoid flying into this kind of cloud because of the high turbulence possible in it. The third main kind of cloud is the **stratus** cloud, which is the lowest type of cloud. A grey stratus cloud usually bears rain.

Study the illustration below to see the relationships of each kind of cloud to the other. Which type do you think is the most dangerous? Which type forms at the highest level? Which type forms at the lowest level? Which ones usually bear rain?

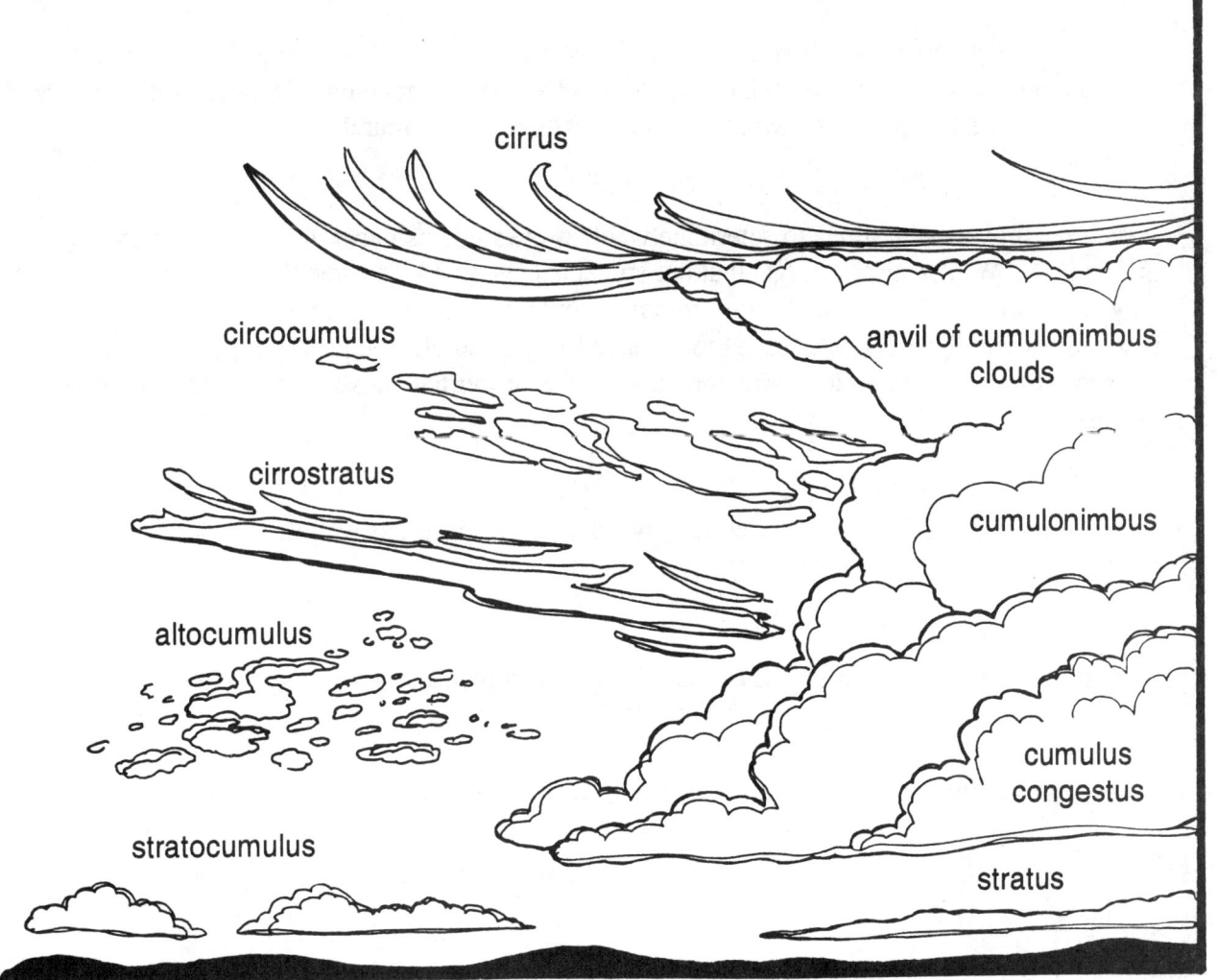

Section 1: First half of "The Gift" *The Red Pony*

Reading Response Journals

Reading response journals can be a very effective means for increasing your students' comprehension and enjoyment of the book. Good readers "get into" their reading, and keeping a daily journal gives them a format for personalizing their reading. Thus, what they read becomes more relevant to their own lives.

This is true even if the lives of the characters in the book are far different from those of the readers. The fact that the setting of the book may be far different from what they see as "real life" today can be a bonus, because the differences between then and now can be used to increase student interest, enabling them to compare and contrast situations.

Using all or even some of the following tips can aid in maximizing the benefits of response journals for your students.

- Give your students a purpose for their reading. Let them know that you consider what they are about to read important and worthwhile.

- Before each day's reading, tell your students what you are going to be asking them to respond to so they can have this idea "in the back of their minds" as they are reading. Knowing ahead will help them write more thoughtful answers. Sample questions can be found on page 44.

- Before reading, ask questions to determine whether the students know important background information. We sometimes forget that our students have lived less time than we have and that they may not be aware of how life was for ordinary people during the time and in the place that the story is set. Surprisingly, many youngsters today take for granted electric power, piped water, and transportation by automobile or airplane. Some of your journal questions may focus on these matters.

- Journals may be used to record vocabulary words and meanings, as well as samples of formal writing.

- If possible, store journals in the classroom. They will stay neater and always be available.

- Allow students time to write; usually five to ten minutes is sufficient.

Section 2: Second half of "The Gift" *The Red Pony*

Quiz Time!

1. On the back of this paper, list three important events in Section 2.

2. How does Gabilan react at first to his training?
   _____
   _____

3. What are some things Billy Buck teaches Jody about "breaking" horses?
   _____
   _____

4. How does Jody practice for the time he will first be able to ride Gabilan?
   _____
   _____

5. What is Billy Buck wrong about, and what happens because of it?
   _____
   _____

6. What does Carl Tiflin hate?
   _____
   _____

7. Describe the pony when Jody finds him in the morning.
   _____
   _____

8. What does Billy Buck call the lump under Gabilan's jaw?
   _____
   _____

9. How does Billy Buck nurse Gabilan?
   _____
   _____

10. Why does Jody kill the buzzard?
    _____
    _____

© 1994 Teacher Created Materials, Inc.   #443 Literature Unit

Section 2: Second half of "The Gift" • The Red Pony

Make a Hair Hygrometer

Billy Buck predicted incorrectly that it was not going to rain, so Jody went off to school leaving Gabilan outside. But Billy was certainly wrong for once, and when Jody returned home, his pony was soaked and cold. It might have been possible for Jody to have had an idea that rain was coming if he had had a hair hygrometer such as the one below.

Have you ever noticed how curly hair is curlier when it is wet? This is because hair is very sensitive to moisture, and it actually becomes longer when it is wet and shorter when it is dry. The moisture or lack of it in the air will cause a change in the hair which can be measured. We can use this fact to make a hair hygrometer which measures the relative humidity in the air by its effect on a human hair.

To make a simple hygrometer you will need the following:

- strand of human hair (Blond works best.)
- toothpick
- glue
- pipe cleaner
- clear wide-mouth drinking glass or jar
- felt-tipped marker or crayon

Directions:

1. Use a human hair longer than the glass is tall. Wrap one end of the hair a few times around the center of the toothpick. Add a drop of glue.

2. Bend the pipe cleaner and fit it across the glass as shown.

3. Holding the toothpick by the hair, hang it on the pipe cleaner inside the jar. Make sure the toothpick hangs just above the bottom of the jar but not touching the sides. With the hair in that position, wrap the free end of the hair around the pipe cleaner at the center and secure it with a drop of glue.

4. After observing the hygrometer over a period of days when it is both fair and rainy, determine the direction the toothpick points during each kind of weather. Use a colored marker or pen to write "clear" or "rainy" positions on the outside of the jar.

Section 2: Second half of "The Gift" *The Red Pony*

Scientific Scavenger Hunt

Form groups of three or four to complete this activity. Take this paper with you from class and "collect" answers as you go through the school day and afterward at home. Ask teachers, parents, neighbors, other students, grandparents, and anyone who might know the answer to one or more questions. On the next school day, come together and share answers with your group. The group collecting the highest number of answers wins.

(Your teacher may approve your locating some information from appropriate reference books if other sources fail.)

Name the following:

1. Theorized the earth circled the sun _____
2. First woman medical doctor in U.S. _____
3. Discovered penicillin _____
4. Discovered the law of gravity _____
5. Science of plants _____
6. Average weather over a period of time _____
7. A chemical element _____
8. Scientific study of animals _____
9. Method used for conducting experiments _____
10. Organisms too small to be seen with the naked eye _____
11. Carries the "blueprint for life" in plants and animals _____
12. Tiny particles which join together to form molecules _____
13. Blanket around earth protecting us from the sun _____
14. Science of the stars _____
15. Disease-causing organisms smaller than bacteria _____
16. Study of how things live in relation to their surroundings _____
17. Ability to make things happen; can be stored _____
18. Light-sensitive cells in the eyes _____

Section 2: Second half of "The Gift" *The Red Pony*

Antibiotics

If the story in *The Red Pony* had occurred today, it might have ended much differently. When Billy Buck lanced the lump which he called "strangles" on the pony's neck and treated the pony's wound with carbolic acid, he gave the pony the best medical treatment he could know about at that time. Carbolic acid (phenol) was an antiseptic solution just strong enough to kill germs without killing the living tissues of a patient, and it was used routinely by doctors. Billy Buck wanted to kill what he knew were "germs" causing the pony to be sick. However the carbolic acid could not go inside the pony's body to kill the bacteria which had entered; it merely stayed on the outside of the pony's wounds. Thus, the pony's infection was not cured, and he died. Antibiotic medicines had not yet been discovered.

The first antibiotic was *penicillin,* which was discovered in 1928, about twenty years after *The Red Pony* takes place. Alexander Fleming, a British scientist, was trying to find an antibacterial medicine—that is, a medicine which would kill bacteria in the body without hurting the body. He had been conducting many experiments with a particular type of bacteria called *staphylococcus,* which is in boils and pimples and which causes several very dangerous illnesses. His discovery of penicillin, however, was almost accidental.

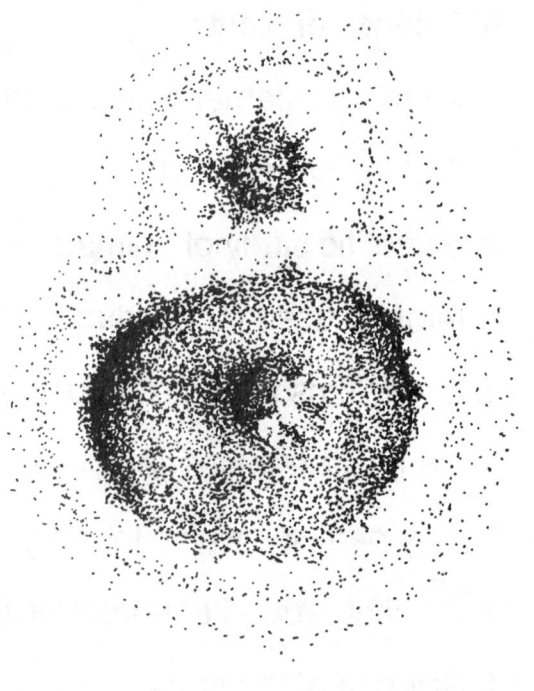

Fleming had gone on a two-week holiday forgetting that several lab dishes containing some colonies of staphylococcus bacteria were lying on the counter near an open window in his laboratory. When he returned, he saw that during his absence a speck of mold had come through the open window and landed in one of the flat dishes. As he studied the contents of the dish, he noted that the staphylococcus near the mold had disappeared or been partly eliminated. The closer the bacteria was to the mold, the thinner it got. Near the mold there was none at all. Fleming was intrigued, and he began further experiments. At the time Fleming discovered penicillin, few people had any idea what a momentous and important discovery it was. There are thousands of molds in the world, many of them in, under, or around a house, for example. Yet this one mold had the ability to kill the bacteria causing some of the most frightening diseases in our world, such as syphilis, staphylococcus infections, and bacterial pneumonia. Fifteen years went by, however, before people recognized the importance of Fleming's discovery. In 1945 Alexander Fleming was finally awarded, along with two other scientists, the Nobel Prize in Medicine.

Activity

Write one or two paragraphs about how Billy Buck's treatment of Gabilan might be different today. Might the story have a different ending? Include facts to back up your opinion. Remember to begin your paper with a topic sentence and wrap up your ending with a conclusion based on facts.

Section 2: Second half of "The Gift" *The Red Pony*

A New Kind of Pioneer

Treating illnesses has changed dramatically since Billy Buck treated Gabilan for an infection. Antibiotics have reduced the numbers of people and animals dying every year from all sorts of infections. And infections are not the only illnesses doctors can now treat successfully.

When your parents and grandparents were children, many people died from illnesses and diseases seldom seen today. Childhood diseases such as measles, mumps, and whooping cough were real killers; and, even when they did not kill, a child was often left with a lifelong problem such as deafness, blindness, or retardation. Medical researchers are today's pioneers as they find new cures and new ways to prevent illness.

I. Survey your parents, grandparents, and any other adults you wish, asking the following questions:

    A. Did you or anyone you know have measles?

    B. Did you or anyone you know have smallpox?

    C. Did you or anyone you know have whooping cough?

    D. Did you or anyone you know have polio?

II. Answer the following questions yourself.

    A. How many of the above diseases have you or anyone you know had?

    B. What kinds of vaccinations have you had?

    C. Name three illnesses common today that you think might be eliminated by the time your children are the age you are now.

    D. If you were a scientist in medical research and you wanted to work on eliminating a terrible disease, what disease would you try to find a cure for?

III. In small groups or as a class discuss the results of your survey.

Section 3: "The Great Mountains" *The Red Pony*

Quiz Time!

1. On the back of this paper, list three important events from Section 3.
2. Why does Jody feel so guilty that he gets a pain in his stomach?
   _____
   _____

3. What does Jody wonder about the mountains?
   _____
   _____

4. What do you know about Gitano?
   _____
   _____

5. How does Carl Tiflin react to the old man?
   _____
   _____

6. Why does the old man come back?
   _____
   _____

7. Who is Easter?
   _____
   _____

8. What does Gitano think of the old horse?
   _____
   _____

9. What precious thing does the old man have?
   _____
   _____

10. What happens to Gitano and Easter?
    _____
    _____

Section 3: "The Great Mountains"   *The Red Pony*

Making a Piñata

Gitano did not say very much during his visit to the Tiflins except that he had been born and raised in the abandoned old adobe house over the hill. If he had talked to Jody about his childhood, however, he would probably have told him about hitting holiday piñatas until candy and small prizes fell out. Hispanic children in Mexico and the American Southwest have enjoyed piñatas for many years, and they remain a favorite activity at parties and on holidays.

You can make your own piñata. It takes a little time, but it is not difficult. To make your piñata you will need the following:

- 16-inch (41 cm) balloon
- one yard (one meter) heavy string
- strips of newspaper
- colored crepe paper
- wallpaper paste
- thinned white latex paint
- poster paint

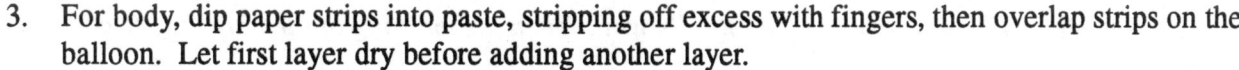

1. Inflate the balloon, tie a knot in the end, and attach the string.

2. Mix wallpaper paste to the consistency of thick pea soup.

3. For body, dip paper strips into paste, stripping off excess with fingers, then overlap strips on the balloon. Let first layer dry before adding another layer.

4. After you have put two or three layers onto the large balloon, tape on additional balloons and cardboard pieces for head, ears, wings, etc. Cover with two or three layers of papier-mâché, letting each layer dry before adding another.

5. Cut a hole in the back and remove the balloon. Use this hole to insert candy and prizes. Fasten a cord at the top to use for hanging.

6. Fringe three-inch-wide (8 cm) strips of colored crepe paper and wrap them around the piñata.

7. Hang the piñata from a high place or from the ceiling. One person at a time is blindfolded and then tries to hit the piñata with a stick. When someone breaks the piñata open, the candy and prizes fall out, and everyone scrambles for the goodies!

 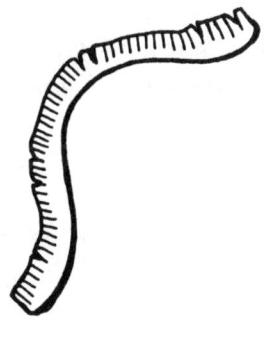 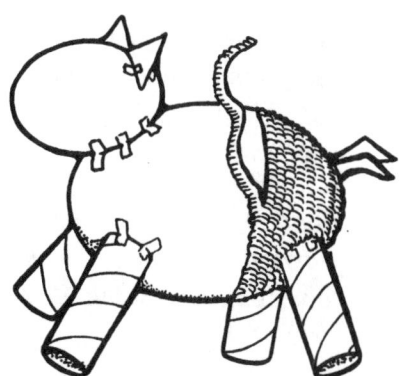

Section 3: "The Great Mountains" *The Red Pony*

Can You Hear Feelings?

Carl Tiflin had a difficult time dealing with his feelings and those of his son. Even when Jody killed the buzzard, his father did not seem able to understand his son's anger that the pony had died. Billy Buck got angry at his boss and said, "Can't you see how he feels?"

Many people grow up not learning how to recognize and deal with their feelings. A person who does not know how to deal with his own feelings often misreads the feelings of other people and, therefore, sometimes misunderstands what others say.

It is possible to learn how to recognize the feelings of others and to articulate them. The following activity can be done by small groups or the whole class, but it should be monitored by a sensitive adult. Remind children that each person's feelings are his own, and feelings, themselves, are not "bad" or "good."

Activity

Explain that in this activity students will listen both to what a person says and to the feelings that person communicates. List on the board some feelings a person might have, then read some of the segments below. After each short segment ask, "What facts did I tell you?" and "What feelings do you think I was telling you about?" Accept divergent, but appropriate, responses. When students are unable to tell you their feelings, explain your feelings to them as a model. There are no "right" or "wrong" answers in this activity, only appropriate or inappropriate.

1. *A terrible thing happened to me last week. I was planning a surprise birthday party for my best friend. I spent a lot of time buying party favors and planning the decorations, and I ordered a super birthday cake. I was so excited I could hardly wait. Then the morning of the party, my friend broke out with chicken pox!*

2. *A couple years ago I started a new hobby—collecting baseball cards. I spend a lot of time going to garage sales and shops which sell baseball cards. Sometimes I even send for them through the mail. Last summer I was really surprised when I learned that two of the cards I'd saved were worth much more than I had originally paid. But even if they weren't worth a lot, I still like collecting them because they are so interesting.*

3. *When I was going on my summer vacation, I packed very carefully. I put all my best clothes, my favorite books, and some really nice gifts for my friends into my suitcase. I checked my suitcase in at the airport. When I arrived at my destination, I looked and looked for my suitcase on the airport carousel, but I couldn't find it anywhere. It hadn't been put on the airplane.*

4. *I went to the movie with my friend the other night. I knew the movie was supposed to be scary, but I hadn't realized just how scary it would turn out to be. All the way home I kept looking behind me to see if someone was following me, and when I got home I double-checked all the doors and windows. I still didn't sleep very well. I kept thinking I heard noises. I don't think I want to see another movie like that!*

5. *I hadn't heard from one of my favorite grandparents for a long time, and I was really getting worried about her. Last night she called to say she was feeling fine and that she would be coming to visit me next week.*

Section 3: "The Great Mountains"   *The Red Pony*

California's Hispanic Legacy

When Gitano arrived at the Tiflin ranch and announced, "I have come back," Jody's mother was confused. She apparently did not know California had a Spanish and Mexican history extending back over 250 years before Jody's birth. That place of history was the place to which Gitano wished to return.

In 1542, under the command of Juan Rodriguez Cabrillo, the Spanish fleet visited California, claiming it for Spain and exploring what is now San Diego Bay. California was far from Spain, however, its gold yet undiscovered, and Spain lost interest in the area for over a hundred years.

By 1763, Spain feared the English might drive from Canada down the western coast to take the rich silver mines in Mexico. Spain planned to erect missions in California, first building crude outposts, then enticing the Native Americans to settle nearby, teaching them Christianity and handcrafts. When they became self-sufficient, the land was to be turned over to them.

Father Junipero Serra and Gaspar de Portola, the governor of Baja (Lower) California, began the exhausting labor of building missions in Alta (Upper) California, starting in San Diego. At first, Serra stayed at San Diego while Portola continued toward Monterey, eventually finding San Francisco Bay. The "Mother Mission" at San Diego Bay began a movement which lasted sixty-six years and saw the building of twenty-one missions.

Mexico achieved independence from Spain in 1821, holding California until it became a territory of the United States in 1848, after the Mexican War. California's Spanish and Mexican heritage has given the state its many Spanish names: San Francisco, Los Angeles, San Jose, San Diego, Santa Cruz, and many more cities, towns, and parks all attest to the state's Spanish-Mexican, Catholic past.

Activity: Jody's home lay between the missions of San Juan Bautista and San Carlos del Carmelo (Carmel). Research one of the California missions and report back to the class either with an oral report or by building a model of your mission. Following is a list of the twenty-one missions and the dates they were founded. Be able to locate them on a California map.

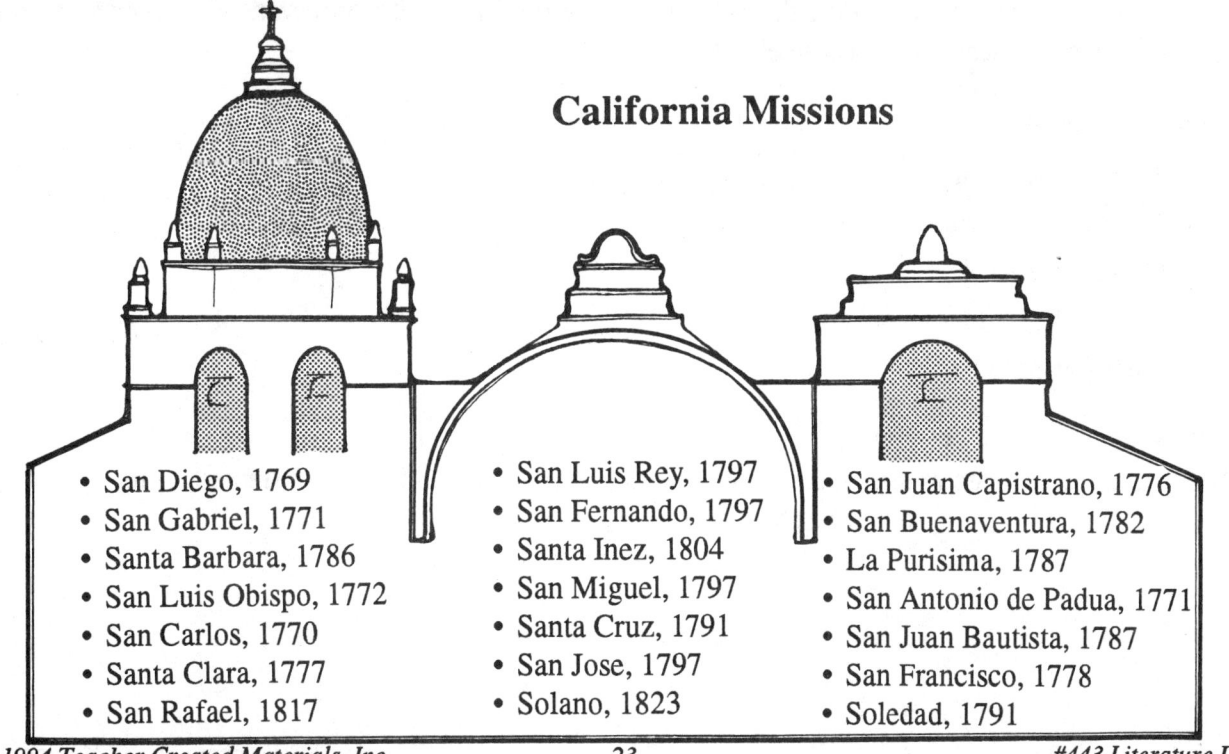

California Missions

- San Diego, 1769
- San Gabriel, 1771
- Santa Barbara, 1786
- San Luis Obispo, 1772
- San Carlos, 1770
- Santa Clara, 1777
- San Rafael, 1817

- San Luis Rey, 1797
- San Fernando, 1797
- Santa Inez, 1804
- San Miguel, 1797
- Santa Cruz, 1791
- San Jose, 1797
- Solano, 1823

- San Juan Capistrano, 1776
- San Buenaventura, 1782
- La Purisima, 1787
- San Antonio de Padua, 1771
- San Juan Bautista, 1787
- San Francisco, 1778
- Soledad, 1791

Section 3: "The Great Mountains" *The Red Pony*

Nonverbal Signs of Listening

Carl Tiflin loved Jody, but he did not always hear what Jody was trying to say to him. Jody's shyness sometimes complicated their communicating with each other as well. Poor listening skills get in the way of understanding what someone else is trying to communicate to you. Remember that clear communication means receiving the message that is sent—that is, it means that you understand the full meaning of what is being said to you. Poor listeners often show their lack of understanding or noninterest by their body language: they may slouch, look around, wiggle, turn sideways, yawn, or drum their fingers on the table.

It is important to learn the nonverbal signs of attention. These include:

- Maintaining good eye contact
- Turning toward the person speaking
- Keeping your fingers and feet still
- Leaning forward a bit toward the speaker
- Appearing interested
- Remaining on the same level as the person with whom you are conversing

Activity

1. In their journals have students write, "When people don't listen to me I feel _____."

2. Then have them write, "When I don't listen to others, they may feel _____."

3. With a student, demonstrate the body signs of good listening; then follow up in a discussion with the class about what took place.

4. Divide the class into groups of three to practice these skills. Take turns with one student being the speaker, another being the listener, and the third being the observer. The observer may list his/her observations in a notebook.

Suggested topics:

- A good dream I had
- A place I would like to visit
- My favorite food
- What I like to do after school
- What I want to be

Follow-up

Direct students to write in their journals, completing the sentence, "I plan to listen better to _____ so that he/she will feel _____."

Section 4: "The Promise"   *The Red Pony*

Quiz Time!

1. On the back of this paper, list three important events in Section 4.

2. Who marches along to school with Jody?
   _____
   _____

3. How does Jody get the horny toad to go to sleep?
   _____
   _____

4. What does Mrs. Tiflin make, and how does she make it?
   _____
   _____

5. Why does Mr. Tiflin "put up" five dollars?
   _____
   _____

6. What does Jody do that makes his mother very unhappy?
   _____
   _____

7. What does Jody have to do to earn the colt?
   _____
   _____

8. Describe Jody's long conversation with Billy Buck about Nellie and the colt.
   _____
   _____

9. How does Jody hurt Billy Buck's feelings?
   _____
   _____

10. What does Billy Buck do to save the colt?
    _____
    _____

Section 4: "The Promise"

Tempting Tapioca

When Mrs. Tiflin serves tapioca pudding for dessert, she serves an old favorite of American children. Tapioca originally came from the root of the cassava plant which grows in Java. It has been such a long-time favorite that it is now processed in the United States.

Tapioca is a versatile product which can be used in many different delicious puddings, but it is also wonderful as a thickener for fruit pies, many kinds of custards, and fruit puddings. Below is a recipe for a basic vanilla tapioca fluff pudding which you can make with your parents at home or with a teacher in your school cooking lab. Remember to always be careful and work safely in a kitchen.

Tapioca Fluff Pudding

You will need the following:

- 3 tablespoons (45 milliliters) tapioca
- ⅓ cup (75 milliliters) sugar
- 2 ¾ cups (675 milliliters) milk
- 1 egg, separated
- 1 teaspoon (5 milliliters) vanilla
- 1 tablespoon (15 milliliters) sugar
- one quart (1 liter) saucepan
- one quart (1 liter) bowl or 6 small pudding dishes
- very small mixing bowl
- egg beater or whip

Combine tapioca and milk in saucepan. Let stand at least 5 minutes. Add sugar and beaten egg yolk. Cook and stir over medium heat until mixture comes just to a boil. Do not overcook pudding, as overcooking will make it sticky. Remove from heat and stir in vanilla.

In a separate small mixing bowl, whip egg white with one tablespoon (15 milliliters) of sugar until stiff. Fold a small amount of the pudding mixture into the beaten egg white, then fold the egg white into the rest of the tapioca pudding.

Chill the pudding. It will thicken as it chills—and then, what a treat!

Variations

You may vary your manner of serving tapioca pudding in many delicious ways. Try one of the following:

- Serve with chocolate sauce or soft chocolate pudding.
- Add melted butter, sauce, sugar, and crushed pineapple to warm pudding.
- Use 2 cups (500 mL) water instead of the milk and add crushed berries.
- Fold sliced fresh peaches or nectarines into warm pudding.
- Decorate with chocolate or strawberry wafer cookies or vanilla wafers.

Section 4: "The Promise" — *The Red Pony*

Honoring the Nobel Winners

In 1895 a wealthy Swedish industrialist named Alfred Nobel established in his will five international awards, including one in literature. This award, generally known as the Nobel Prize for Literature, was to be given each year to "the person who shall have produced in the field of literature the most outstanding work of an idealistic tendency," and it was to be given by the Swedish Academy in Stockholm, Sweden. The Nobel Prize includes a large cash award, but the prestige gained by the person who receives it is even greater than the monetary value.

The first Nobel Prize for Literature was given in 1901. Between that date and 1962, only seven Americans received it. John Steinbeck, the author of *The Red Pony*, was one. An author honored by this greatest of all literary awards has generally published many books, stories, or poems over a considerable period of time, and the award recognizes their continuing contributions to literature.

The Red Pony, first published in 1933, is considered to be one of Steinbeck's very best works. It is not exactly a novel in the sense of being one rather long story. Instead, it is a collection of four stories recalling Steinbeck's own childhood during the very early 1900's, (He was born in 1902.) and his growth through sometimes painful experiences to become a compassionate adult. The book also shows the relationships among three generations in a family: Jody, Jody's father Carl Tiflin, and Jody's grandfather.

John Steinbeck wrote many novels, and he was first nominated for the Nobel Prize in 1945. He did not receive the award until 1962, after he had written many stories and novels. Some other especially good works of Steinbeck's before 1962 included *Of Mice and Men*, *The Grapes of Wrath*, and *The Pearl*.

Activity

In groups of three or four choose one of the following names of the six American authors who, in addition to John Steinbeck, were honored with the Nobel Prize for Literature:

Sinclair Lewis (1885-1951) won in 1930.   T.S. Eliot (1888-1965) won in 1948.

Eugene O'Neill (1888-1953) won in 1936.   William Faulkner (1897-1962) won in 1949.

Pearl Buck (1892-1973) won in 1938.   Ernest Hemingway (1898-1961) won in 1954.

Prepare an author sketch to present to the rest of the class telling who your author is, the outstanding works written by your author, and what distinguishes your author from others. Give a summary of one of your author's books, plays, or poems.

Section 4: "The Promise"   *The Red Pony*

The Salinas Valley

The map shows that the Salinas River runs southeast from Monterey almost parallel to the western coastline of the Pacific Ocean. However, you might have trouble finding it unless you visit during or shortly after the rainy season. The river bed runs through the Long Valley, almost one hundred miles long, known to most people as the Salinas Valley. If you drive about ten or twelve miles almost due west from the town of Salinas, you will find yourself in the coastal town of Monterey. Drive the same distance in the opposite direction, and you will see the grandfather of California earthquake fractures, the San Andreas fault, which runs right through the grounds of the San Juan Bautista Mission.

John Steinbeck said in *Travels With Charley* that the Salinas of his childhood was "a little town, a general store under a tree, and a blacksmith shop." Four thousand people lived there then. Well over a hundred thousand live there now, and many more come in from neighboring farm towns to shop in the mall.

Highway 101, a major north-south route running from Washington state through Los Angeles, now runs through Salinas, but in the fertile soil of the valley still grows much of the produce that feeds America. Lettuce, broccoli, Brussels sprouts, and strawberries thrive there, and the valley is often called the Salad Bowl of the World. Smaller farming towns nearby have given themselves grandiose nicknames, such as, "The Garlic Capital of the World," and "The Artichoke Capital of the World." Salinas, itself, has each year one of the world's largest rodeos.

Here in this long bowl of the valley nestled between the Gabilan Mountains to the east and the Santa Lucia Mountains to the west, one hundred miles south of San Francisco and near enough to the sea to observe occasional seagulls, John Steinbeck set most of his greatest works, including *The Red Pony*.

Steinbeck wrote about the land and the people who worked the land. In one way, he never really left the town of his birth, for the people and places he wrote about were mostly there, as was Jody. Salinas stayed in Steinbeck's memory as a small town surrounded by ranches and filled with the people of childhood. In his mind, he never wanted it to change.

On the map, find the setting for *The Red Pony*. In which directions lie the following: the Pacific Ocean, Salinas River, Gabilan Mountains, Monterey Bay, and the Santa Lucia Mountains?

Section 4: "The Promise"   *The Red Pony*

Present a Literary Award

This is your chance to nominate your favorite author for an award. Your award's name can be called "The Steinbeck Young Reader's Award," or any other name you and your classmates choose. Think carefully about your reasons for nominating your author and consider the whole body of literature which your author has written. When you complete the nomination form below, turn it in to your teacher. When the class has finished the reading of *The Red Pony*, you can meet together as a literary academy and choose the author you consider the best one from the group of nominees.

Official Nomination

Author's name _____

Dates of birth and death _____

Country of citizenship _____

Literature type _____

Representative works of literature by this author _____

_____

_____

Reasons for nominating this author (Be specific.) _____

_____

_____

_____

_____

_____

Signed

_____

Section 5: "The Leader of the People"   *The Red Pony*

Quiz Time!

1. On the back of this paper, list three important events in Section 5.

2. What does Jody want to hunt?
   _____
   _____

3. Who is the letter to Mrs. Tiflin from?
   _____
   _____

4. Why does Carl Tiflin not like Jody's grandfather to visit?
   _____
   _____

5. Describe Jody's grandfather.
   _____
   _____

6. How does Billy Buck's father get his name?
   _____
   _____

7. What does Grandfather say people would do when they ran out of food?
   _____
   _____

8. What is "westering"?
   _____
   _____

9. Grandfather believes he did one important thing in his life. What is it?
   _____
   _____

10. How does Jody see his grandfather—that is, in what ways does Jody think of him and relate to him?
    _____
    _____

Section 5: "The Leader of the People" *The Red Pony*

Build a Covered Wagon

To build a model of a covered wagon such as the one Grandfather might have used when he led the people, you will need the following:

- shoebox or similar cardboard box
- wire or bamboo strips for ribs of top, 28 inches (71 cm) each
- craft stick for the wagon tongue
- four wheels cut from pasteboard, 4 to 5 inches (10 to 13 cm) in diameter
- eight paper fasteners
- paper punch and nail for poking holes in wheels and wagon body
- cloth for cover
- glue
- scissors
- poster paint

Cut boxtop as indicated by dotted lines. Keep aside one piece, 1 ½ inch (4 cm) wide, and glue on as shown for seat. Use the other piece of 2 ¾ inches (7 cm) as a footrest and glue on beneath seat as shown. With paper fasteners, attach wheels to front and back sides. Glue craft stick at front to serve as tongue. Bend wire or bamboo strips over from one side to the other for ribs. Insert ends into holes in each side of the wagon body. Paint wagon. When wagon is dry, cut cloth to fit over ribs as cover. Attach to the wagon body with paper fasteners.

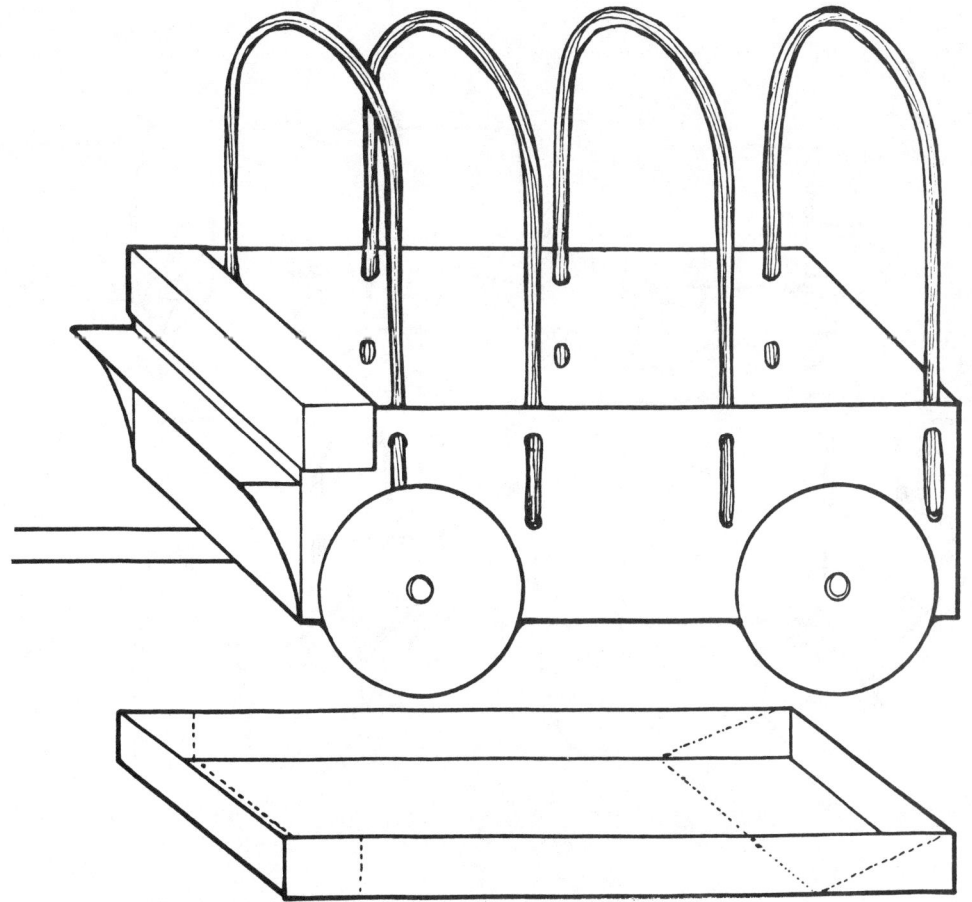

© 1994 Teacher Created Materials, Inc.

Section 5: "The Leader of the People"　　　　　　　　　　　　　　*The Red Pony*

Build a Corral

The westward movement, or "westering" as Grandfather called it, was a long time coming from the days when New England was first settled by Europeans. To people coming from Europe, where open space was much smaller, the land we now call the continental United States must have appeared vast beyond belief, and except for scattered tribes of Native Americans and a few Spaniards who came up into the southwest from Mexico, few people had made it west of the Mississippi River. But once people started "westering," they didn't stop, despite the many hardships it brought.

Grandfather "led the people" in a wagon train, and he tells and retells his story about how the wagons were all put into a circle when the wagon train stopped at night. Horses, cattle, and people stayed inside the circle, and if they were attacked by unfriendly Native Americans, this circle, called a corral, afforded a modicum of protection. While women and children stayed out of sight, the men would hide behind the wheels and defend the wagon train by shooting at the Native Americans who usually rode in circles around the corral.

Activity

With six to ten of your classmates, build a corral. Use the model covered wagons you have made (page 31) and your imagination. You will need a large piece of cardboard or plywood to put it on, or if a spare table is available, you could use the table top. If anyone in your group has small plastic figures of people, you may place them in or around your corral, or you may make small people from craft sticks, pipe cleaners, and other materials. Your corral will make an interesting display for back-to-school night or any other time parents and friends come to school to visit.

Section 5: "The Leader of the People"   *The Red Pony*

Descriptive Writing

John Steinbeck was a master at writing descriptions. Whether he was describing people or places, his readers can actually see with their "mind's eye" the person or place Steinbeck wants them to see. Read the first paragraph of *The Red Pony*. Within that paragraph the readers learn more than just what Billy Buck looks like. The readers also see the kind of person Billy Buck was, what he did for a living, and what some of his daily habits were.

Steinbeck gave his readers a tremendous amount of information about one person within one single paragraph.

You, too, can learn to describe a person or place so that others can "see." There is no magic involved in writing a good description, but it does take some work.

First, you need to read as much good writing as possible; *The Red Pony* is a good start. If you enjoy Steinbeck, you might wish to try *Travels with Charley* later.

Second, really look at the first paragraph in *The Red Pony* in which Steinbeck described Billy Buck. Notice the words used to tell what Billy Buck looked like: *broad, bandy-legged, square hands, muscled on the palms, wearing blue jeans, eyes were a contemplative, watery grey*, as a start. Then notice words used to tell what Billy Buck did: he *emerged from the bunkhouse, looked at the sky, cleared each nostril, walked to the barn, curried and brushed two saddle horses*, and *he moved with deliberate action which was wasteless of time*.

Next, read two or three more pages and notice the things that Billy Buck said—for example, his explanation to the little boy of why there was a spot of blood on his egg yolk and that it would not hurt him. This is something a caring parent might well say to a child.

Now that you have really studied Steinbeck's words and the way he described Billy Buck, you are ready to try writing a description of your own.

Activity: Writing a Description of a Person

1. Choose someone you know very well as the subject of your description. You can always write much better if you write about what you know.

2. On a piece of paper, plan your description by first making lists under the following headings:

    What this person looks like *(physical description)*

    What this person does *(actions)*

    What this person says

    What other people think about this person

3. Now, referring to the lists you have made, write a paragraph describing your subject. Using the best choice of words you can, draw a word picture of your person which makes him or her a living, breathing, acting individual.

Important Note: Just as with any other skill, remember the old saying, "Practice makes perfect!" In your spare time, keep a diary and write letters, stories, and/or poems.

Section 5: "The Leader of the People" *The Red Pony*

Become a Book Illustrator!

A book illustrator has the very important job of interpreting a story, then drawing pictures to show how certain scenes may have looked. Each illustrator will have his or her own interpretation of how each scene would look, just as each reader will. This is your chance to use your own artistic ability to show your individual idea of how a scene in *The Red Pony* would look.

Think about the scene where Grandfather tells about his idea of a new way to protect the wagon train from unfriendly Native Americans. Draw your interpretation of the way you think the wagons would look and how they would shield the people from flying arrows.

After the Book | The Red Pony

Any Questions?

When you finished reading *The Red Pony*, did you have any questions about the characters that were unanswered? Write some of your questions here.

_____
_____
_____
_____
_____
_____

Working in groups, or by yourself, prepare possible answers for some or all of the questions you have asked above and those written below. When you have finished your predictions, share your answers with the class.

- When Jody grew up, did he stay on the ranch where he was born and raised, or did he go off to another part of the world as John Steinbeck did and never come back to live in the place of his birth? Did he become a rancher like his father? Or did he find a way to use his rich imagination in a creative and productive way, such as writing or painting?

- Did Jody ever get to ride in the Salinas rodeo? If so, was it on the horse that the little black colt grew into? Did he ever ride the horse in a parade? Did the horse grow up to become a stallion or a mare?

- Where did Gitano go when he went up into the mountains? How long did he and Easter live? Did he go back to the worn-down house where he was born? Stealing a horse was a serious crime. Why did Carl Tiflin not go after Gitano and bring back the horse?

- Did Jody ever get to go across the mountains? If so, when did he go, and what did he think when he saw what was there? Why did Grandfather believe that once they got to the ocean, there was no place else to go? Do you think that the appetite for "westering" had died? Are there no frontiers left for people to explore? If there are, what are they? Do they have to be frontiers of the land, or are there other frontiers?

- Did Jody ever go on his mouse hunt? Why would he think it was exciting to chase mice out of the haystack? Did he ever go on another kind of hunt?

- Did Jody and his father ever get to the point where they could really talk to each other? Did Mr. Tiflin ever learn how to deal with or express his feelings?

After the Book   *The Red Pony*

Book Report Ideas

There are almost as many ways to report on a book as there are books to report on. You may report as a group with one or more of your classmates. You may choose to write your own traditional written or oral report, you may think of an idea of your own, or you may choose one of the following ideas:

- **Write an autobiographical story.**

The Red Pony is an autobiographical novel— that is, Steinbeck wrote about his life as a young boy on a California ranch in the early 1900's. He used his own sometimes painful experiences to show how a child might grow through those experiences and to show the relationship between life and death. Write your own autobiographical story based in some way on your own experiences.

- **Paint your wagon!**

Build a model covered wagon like the ones Jody's grandfather would have led on his westering journey. Research the design of famous covered wagons, and build your wagon to scale.

- **Invent a game.**

Make up your own idea for a game based on a part of *The Red Pony*. For example, your game might have a wild west theme having to do with a wagon train. It might have a ranch theme, having to do with animals and weather. Or it might be based on schools in the old west. Make the marker or pieces needed to play the game, and teach it to your classmates.

- **Stage a skit.**

Together with one or more classmates, write and produce a skit which dramatizes an important scene from the book. To make your skit more real to the people watching it, design some stage effects and costumes which recall the time and place in which the story takes place.

- **Extend your reading.**

Read another novel by Steinbeck or a novel with a similar or related setting, such as one from the bibliography of related readings. Write a report comparing and contrasting the books.

- **Design an advertising poster.**

Using bright colors and your best imagination, make a poster to persuade others to read *The Red Pony*. Choose something from the book which symbolizes it for you, and incorporate that symbol into your design.

- **Interview the author.**

Together with a classmate, prepare an interview which a television reporter might have had with John Steinbeck. For this you will have to research statements made by the author or things he wrote during his lifetime so your interview will be accurate and truly like what he might have answered.

- **Change the point of view.**

The Red Pony was written from the point of view of Jody. How would the story be told from the point of view of another character? Rewrite the story, or part of it, from the viewpoint of, for example, the pony, Billy Buck, Gitano, or Carl Tiflin. Or how would Mrs. Tiflin see the story differently?

- **Write a fable.**

Write a fable using Gabilan, Nellie, or the colt as your main character. Remember that in a fable, animals talk and act like humans. You must also include setting and plot, and use your fable to illustrate a moral or lesson.

- **Write a poem.**

Write a poem about a character or event in *The Red Pony*.

After The Book   The Red Pony

Research Ideas

Describe three things in *The Red Pony* that you would like to learn more about.

1. _____

2. _____

3. _____

As you read *The Red Pony*, you encountered a part of the United States and a way of life you may never have known about before. The book includes many events, procedures, ideas, beliefs, lifestyles, and even a writing style which may seem strange to you. Understanding these things will help to increase your understanding of the book. It will also help you to fully appreciate John Steinbeck's remarkable craft as a writer.

Work in groups or on your own to research one or more of the areas you named above or the areas named below. Share what you learn with the rest of the class in either a report or project.

- Horses
    - training
    - breeding
    - shoeing
    - the first horses
    - judging
    - racing
    - famous race horse
- Veterinary medicine
- Horseless carriages
- Farming
- Horned toads
- Pioneer cooking
- Spanish California
- History of California
- California Native Americans
- The Salinas Rodeo
- Western medical practices
- Childhood diseases
- The weather
- Shetland ponies
- California geography
- Diseases of horses
- Infections

- The Westward Movement
    - wagon trains
    - cowboys
    - Native Americans
    - frontier towns
    - famous trails
    - corrals
    - Frontier law
- Rodeos
- Famous gunfighters
- Milk production
- Wood stoves
- Cooking on the trail
- Frontier schools
- The Mexican War
- The Salinas Valley
- John Steinbeck's novels
- Antibiotics
- Mule trains
- California weather
- Clouds
- Birds of prey
- Buzzards and vultures
- Pneumonia

Culminating Activity   *The Red Pony*

Old West Day

Some of the most exciting days of Jody's life were those when his grandfather came to visit. Jody loved to listen to the old man's tales of how he led the people in a wagon train to California, braving the wilderness and unfriendly Native Americans. Jody longed to someday lead the people himself, although Grandfather told him it was too late. Life on the trail was difficult, and only hardy people were able to complete it. These people became heroes to Jody and to many others, as well. The Old West still holds an attraction for many people, and many movies and television shows have been filmed about it.

A fun way to celebrate the reading of *The Red Pony* would be to have an Old West celebration with food, games, and exhibits. Suggestions of games and food for your celebration are on the following pages, and ideas for sharing the many enjoyable projects you have undertaken are listed below.

Write handwritten invitations to those people you would like to invite to your celebration: parents, other classrooms, and school staff. Write them in pen and ink, using your best writing; then fold them and drip melted wax onto the seam, pressing your "seal" onto the wax to flatten it. Deliver your invitations personally.

On Old West Day wear western clothing and use candles instead of electric lights. Really enjoy this time you have together. Here are some ideas for exhibitions and events for Old West Day.

Displays
- Vocabulary projects
- Knotting projects (page 11)
- Hair hygrometers (page 16)
- Models of California missions (page 23)
- Tapioca pudding (page 26)
- Covered wagons and corrals (pages 31 and 32)
- Book illustrations (page 34)
- Old Western Music

Events
- Play some of the games described on page 40.
- Demonstrate knotting.
- Go on a scientific scavenger hunt (page 17)
- Hit piñatas for fun and prizes (page 21).
- Enjoy an Old West picnic (page 39).
- Announce the winner of the Literary Award (pages 27 and 29).
- Present research findings (page 37).
- Demonstrate dances common in the Old West, such as square dances or the Virginia Reel.

Culminating Activity *The Red Pony*

Old West Day (cont.)

Chuckwagon Food

Food eaten during the journey of a wagon train in frontier America was, by necessity, very simple. There were no "convenience foods" such as we take for granted, no refrigerators or freezers, and there were no grocery stores along the way. The only fresh foods to be had were wild fruits, nuts, berries, and sometimes freshly killed game. If the traveling family was more affluent than most, they might have had a milk cow or two for fresh milk and butter.

Often an animal on which a family had depended, however, died during the trip from exhaustion, lack of sufficient food and water, or from an Native American arrow or bullet. Since the journey would take many weeks—probably months—a family needed to take large amounts of food along, particularly flour, corn meal, dried beans, salt, and other staple goods, and these foods had to be rationed to last the entire journey. There would be little room left for clothes, toys, or nonessentials.

Some suggestions for your chuckwagon lunch are below. If your school has facilities for barbecuing or heating food, you are in luck, and you can have hamburgers and beans. Otherwise you can bring sandwiches, fresh vegetables and dip, and fruit to school and still have a chuckwagon picnic. Serve food from a table decorated with brown paper to look like a covered wagon. Either way you do it, this is a great way to celebrate the reading of *The Red Pony*!

Hamburgers

You will need for each serving:
- hamburger patty
- hamburger bun
- pickles or relish
- mustard
- catsup

Grill patties on barbecue or a stove. Serve patties on buns adding condiments as desired.

Zippy Vegetables and Dip

You will need:
- fresh vegetable pieces, washed and chilled
- dip made of 1 package dried onion soup mix and 1 pint (500 millileters) sour cream mixed together.

Humdinger Apples

You will need:
- fresh apples cut into halves or quarters
- peanut butter

Spread peanut butter on crisp apple pieces. Mmm good!

Campfire Beans

You will need for eight servings:
- 1 pound (480 grams) ground beef
- 1 onion, if desired
- 1 packet dried chili seasoning
- one 14 ounce (420 grams) can tomatoes
- two 14 ounce (420 grams) cans kidney beans

Brown ground beef and drain fat. Stir in remaining ingredients. Cover and simmer for at least ten minutes.

Culminating Activity   *The Red Pony*

Old West Day (cont.)

Games, Games, Games

People everywhere play games. Sometimes these games are very complicated and involve a lot of equipment. Other games are simple, requiring little in the way of necessary materials.

Children traveling west in a wagon train had to be satisfied with simple games because space on the wagons was needed for carrying clothes, food, and things needed to begin a new home. As part of your Old West Day, organize some of the following games.

Keep Away

Divide players into two teams. Draw straws to see which team begins the game. The players on the beginning team pass the ball or other object between themselves, trying to keep the other team from getting it. They score a point for each completed pass from one player to another on the same team. The other team tries to get the object, and when it does, it tries to keep it as the first team did. Play goes on for a set period of time, after which the team having the most completed passes wins.

Ante Over

Divide players into two teams, and one team gets on each side of a basketball hoop or swing set. A rubber ball or bean bag is given to a player on one team. He/she shouts, "Ante over!" and throws the ball or bean bag high over the hoop or swing set. (It must go directly over to count.) A player on the other team tries to catch the ball or bean bag. He/she then runs around to the other side and tries to hit any member of the other team with it. If he/she is successful, the player he/she hits becomes a member of his/her team. If no one catches the ball or bean bag, any player who retrieves it throws it back over, calling, "Ante over!" Game continues until all players are on one team.

Steal the Bacon

An object, such as a bean bag or bowling pin is the "bacon" and is placed in the middle of the playing area. A group is divided into two teams which line up facing each other. Each team counts off in line in opposite directions. The teacher calls a number, and players from each side having that number run to the center and try to get the "bacon." The player getting it runs back to his/her team while trying not to get tagged by the other player. If he/she is tagged, the team getting the "bacon" gets a point. If he/she is not tagged, his/her team gets two points.

Fox and Chickens

All players except one line up. The first in line is the "hen," and the rest of the line members are "chicks." The other player is the "fox." When the signal is given, the "fox" starts around the line and tries to catch the last "chick." The mother "hen" flaps her wings and follows the "fox," trying to keep him from getting the "chick." The other "chicks" turn away and follow the "hen," their hands on the waist of the one in front of them. When a "chick" is caught, he joins the "fox." Game continues until all the "chicks" are caught.

Broomstick Wrestle

Two players face each other, holding tight to a broomstick. Their hands should be about 18 inches (½ meter) apart. When given a signal, each player tries to cause the other player to move his/her feet. The one to win is the first player to cause the other to move his/her feet.

Unit Test: Option 1   The Red Pony

Objective Test and Essay

Matching: Match the descriptions of the characters with their names.

1. _____ Gitano   A. was a mean devil sometimes
2. _____ Billy Buck   B. always limped when he was hurt
3. _____ Jody   C. died giving birth
4. _____ Gabilan   D. had a lot of trouble dealing with feelings
5. _____ Mrs. Tiflin   E. had led the people
6. _____ Nellie   F. came back to where he was born
7. _____ Jess Taylor   G. the son of a mule packer
8. _____ Carl Tiflin   H. felt caught between Carl and Grandfather
9. _____ Easter   I. had a very rich fantasy life
10. _____ Mutt   J. was a first for Carl Tiflin
11. _____ Grandfather   K. gave the boy two pieces of pie
12. _____ Sundog   L. had pneumonia and strangles

True or False: Answer true or false in the blanks below.

1. _____ Billy Buck was always right.
2. _____ Jody and his father often had a poor understanding of each other.
3. _____ Grandfather led three wagon trains across the country.
4. _____ Gitano took his rifle when he went into the mountains.
5. _____ Grandfather was Jody's hero.

Short Answer: Write a brief response to each question in the space provided.

1. Who made a hackamore for Jody? _____
2. What did Billy Buck do to help Jody train Gabilan?_____
3. What is the setting of *The Red Pony?* _____
4. How did Carl Tiflin feel about Grandfather? _____
5. Why did Grandfather stop leading the people?_____

Essay: Respond to the following on the back of this paper.

The relationships between Jody and his grandfather, and between Jody and Billy Buck are very different from the relationship between Jody and his father. Describe the relationship which Jody has with each of the three men in his life. Could those relationships have been any different? What might have made them different?

Essay Challenge: Include in your essay your definition of love and how it was shown in these relationships.

Unit Test: Option 2   *The Red Pony*

Response

Explain the meaning of these quotations from *The Red Pony*.

Section 1

'But, Ruth, I didn't give much for him.'

Before today Jody had been a boy, dressed in overalls and a blue shirt—quieter than most, even suspected of being a little cowardly. And now he was different.

'Have you forgot the wood-box?' she asked gently. 'It's not far off from dark and there's not a stick of wood in the house, and the chickens aren't fed.'

'It takes all the dignity out of a horse to make him do tricks.'

Section 2

'Now when you get up there, just grab tight with your knees and keep your hands away from the saddle, and if you get throwed, don't let that stop you.'

'Not likely to rain today. She's rained herself out.'

Jody looked reproachfully at Billy Buck and Billy felt guilty.

He struck again and again, until the buzzard lay dead, until its head was a red pulp.

'Man, can't you see how he'd feel about it?'

Section 3

Jody knew something was there, something very wonderful because it wasn't known, something secret and mysterious.

'I have come back,' the old man said.

'Too old to work,' Gitano repeated. 'Just eats and pretty soon dies.'

For a moment he thought he could see a black speck crawling up the farthest ridge.

Section 4

'I'll put up the money, but you'll have to work it out all summer.'

Billy knew he had been infallible before that, and now he was capable of failure.

When Jody rode the black horse to the starting chute the other contestants shrugged and gave up first place.

'You won't let anything happen, Billy, you're sure you won't?'

Section 5

'I just wonder whether I ever told you how those thieving Piutes drove off thirty-five of our horses.'

'All right! Now it's finished. Nobody wants to hear about it over and over.'

'The westering was as big as God—Then we came to the sea, and it was done.'

Unit Test: Option 3 — The Red Pony

Conversations

In size-appropriate groups, write and perform the conversation that might have occurred in one of the following situations. If you wish, you may use your own conversation idea for characters from *The Red Pony*.

- Jody, as an adult, tells his grandson about how Grandfather led the people cross country in a wagon train.

- Jody overcomes his shyness enough to tell his father how he feels about Gabilan's death.

- Billy Buck and Jody discuss how it feels to lose someone or something you love.

- Gitano tells Jody what it was like to grow up in the adobe house when California was Hispanic.

- Mr. and Mrs. Tiflin discuss Jody's getting another horse.

- Mr. Tiflin and Billy Buck talk about young boys and how to raise them.

- Jody confesses to Billy Buck that he killed the bird.

- Two of Jody's friends talk together about Jody's new pony.

- Jody explains to Grandfather why he wants to see the ocean and what lies over the mountains.

- Grandfather describes for Jody the best kind of covered wagon and how to build it.

- Billy Buck explains to Jody that everything eventually dies.

- Jody's grandson, who is now a college student, tells the old Jody about the new antibiotics, vaccinations, and "miracle" drugs.

- Jody confesses to Billy Buck his dreams for riding in the rodeo.

- Grandfather describes his journey across the country by wagon train to a classroom of students and answers their questions.

- Gitano tells Jody the story of how his father came to have the beautiful rapier.

- Billy Buck explains to Mr. Tiflin why he killed Nellie.

Journal — The Red Pony

Journal Questions

Section 1 and 2: "The Gift"
1. What kind of boy is Jody, and how can you tell?
2. How could Jody tell that his father and Billy Buck had a secret?
3. What did Jody's friends think about the gift he had received?
4. How did Billy Buck teach Jody to care for the pony?
5. How did Jody prepare for the day he would be allowed to ride Gabilan?
6. How did the pony react to Jody's halter-training him?
7. What instructions did Billy Buck give Jody about training Gabilan?
8. How did Billy Buck care for the sick pony?
9. Why did Jody feel guilty about the pony being sick?
10. Why did Jody kill the buzzard?
11. What did Jody think about Billy Buck, and why was he disappointed in him?

Section 3: "The Great Mountains"
1. What did Jody do which made him feel guilty?
2. How does Carl Tiflin react to Jody's wanting to go over the mountains?
3. Describe Gitano.
4. Why would Carl Tiflin not keep the old man on the ranch to work?
5. Why did Gitano not go to his relatives?
6. How were Gitano and Easter like each other?
7. What happened to the old man and the old horse?

Section 4: "The Promise"
1. What wild game did Jody hunt, and how did his mother react to what he did with it?
2. What did Billy Buck tell Mr. Tiflin about Jody, and why is it important to Jody?
3. Why did Nellie become complacent, and how did she act?
4. In what ways did Billy Buck mean you could never trust a stallion?
5. How did Billy Buck now feel he was capable of failure, and why?
6. Describe Jody's daydream.
7. What did Billy Buck mean when he said he was "half horse myself"?
8. What special care did Jody give Nellie as the winter wore on?
9. Why did Billy Buck kill Nellie?

Section 5: "The Leader of the People"
1. How did Jody plan to hunt mice?
2. Why was Carl Tiflin unhappy that Jody's grandfather was coming to visit?
3. How did Jody feel about his grandfather?
4. How did Billy Buck feel about Grandfather?
5. What stories did Grandfather tell about people running out of food on the road west?
6. What was Grandfather's story about his unusual idea for protecting the wagon train from Indians?
7. What was "westering"?
8. What was important to Grandfather about westering?
9. Why did Grandfather think that Jody would never be able to "lead the people" as he had done?

The Red Pony

Bibliography of Related Readings

Resource Materials

Boy Scouts of America. *Knots and How to Tie Them.* (Irving, Texas, 1991)

Boy Scouts of America. *Weather.* (Irving, Texas, 1992)

Cihak, Mary and Heron, Barbara J. *Games Children Should Play.* (Goodyear Publishing Co., Inc., 1980)

French, Warren G. and Kidd, Walter E. *American Winners of the Nobel Literary Prize.* (University of Oklahoma Press, 1968)

Lavender, David. *California: A Bicentennial History.* (W.W. Norton & Company, Inc. 1976)

Macfarlane, Gwyn. *Alexander Fleming: The Man and the Myth.* (Harvard University Press, 1984)

Pourade, Richard F. *Time of the Bells.* (The Union-Tribune Publishing Company, 1961)

Random House. *The Random House Basic Dictionary, Spanish.* (Ballantine Books, 1981)

Random House. *The Random House Children's Encyclopedia.* (Random House, 1991)

Rombauer, Irma S. and Becker, Marion Rombauer. *The Joy of Cooking.* (The Bobbs-Merrill Company, Inc., 1953)

Steinbeck, John. *Travels with Charley.* (The Viking Press, Inc., 1962)

Weight Watchers. *Meals in Minutes Cookbook.* (New American Library, Penguin Books USA Inc., 1989)

Fiction

Borland, Hal. *When the Legends Die.* (Lippincott, 1963)

Craven, Margaret. *I Heard the Owl Call My Name.* (Doubleday, 1973)

Farley, Walter. *The Black Stallion.* (Random House, 1944)

Highwater, Jamake. *Legend Days.* (Harper Collins, 1984)

O'Hara, Mary. *My Friend Flicka.* (Lippincott, 1973)

Rawlings, Marjorie K. *The Yearling.* (Scribner, 1962)

Rawls, Wilson. *Where the Red Fern Grows.* (Bantam, 1985)

Schaefer, Jack. *Shane.* (Houghton Mifflin, 1954)

Teacher Aids/Audio-Visual

Cassette: *The Red Pony.* Read by Eli Wallach. (Caedmon, New York)

Center for Literary Review Sound filmstrip. *The Red Pony and "Discussion Guide for the Novel."* (Cassettes Unlimited, Roanoke, Texas)

Filmstrip: A Sound Filmstrip Program with Study Guide—*The Red Pony.* (Media Basics, New York, 1981)

Special Credit

The author of this unit would like to give very special thanks to Mary Gamble, archivist at the Steinbeck Library in Salinas, California, for the considerable amount of time she spent helping with research for this unit. She shared a great deal of knowledge about Steinbeck and shared family photos and tapes to allow for a more in-depth treatment of *The Red Pony* than would otherwise have been possible.

The Red Pony

Answer Key

Quiz Time Section 1: First half of "The Gift" (page 10)
1. Accept appropriate responses.
2. Accept responses describing the Tiflin's ranch home.
3. The ranch hand who works for the Tiflins.
4. Stern, strong disciplinarian, doesn't show his feelings.
5. A pony.
6. He had to wait to ride the pony because the pony was too young for riding.
7. They were full of admiration and questions, wanting to ride him someday.
8. All about horses.
9. Tail hair to braid into a hair rope or hackamore.
10. Carl Tiflin thought the things Jody was teaching the pony to do made him look like a trick pony.

Quiz Time Section 2: Second half of "The Gift" (page 15)
1. Accept appropriate responses.
2. He hunched and reared and threw the saddle off. He fought the bridle until his mouth bled. He was afraid and became rambunctious.
3. How to sit on the horse and hold him, and if he was thrown, to get right back on until the horse would let him ride.
4. He listened carefully to all Billy Buck told him. He practiced on the sawhorse, and he began putting his weight on the stirrup but did not throw his leg over.
5. Billy Buck said it would not rain so Jody left Gabilan outside when he left for school, and the pony got wet and cold.
6. Weakness, sickness, and helplessness.
7. He had a hollow, rasping cough. His eyes were half closed with crusty mucus. Fluid ran from his nostrils, and he did not respond to Jody.
8. Strangles.
9. He put a canvas nose bag on Gabilan with bran, hops, carbolic acid, turpentine, and hot water in it to "steam" him and, Billy covered him with a blanket. Then he cut open the lump to drain it and put salve on it. When this was not enough, he cut a hole in the pony's throat to allow him to breathe.
10. Accept appropriate answers which show understanding that Jody was taking out his anger at Gabilan's death on another animal, even though that animal had not caused his pony to die.

Cooperative Activity: Scientific Scavenger Hunt (page 17)
1. Copernicus
2. Elizabeth Blackwell
3. Alexander Fleming
4. Isaac Newton
5. Botany
6. Climate
7. Any element from the Periodic Table
8. Zoology
9. Scientific Method
10. Microorganisms
11. DNA
12. Atoms
13. Atmosphere
14. Astronomy
15. Viruses
16. Ecology
17. Energy
18. Rods and cones

The Red Pony

Answer Key (cont.)

Quiz Time Section 3: "The Great Mountains" (page 20)
1. Accept appropriate responses.
2. He felt guilty about killing the bird and cutting it up.
3. He wondered what lay beyond them.
4. Accept appropriate responses which describe or accurately apply to Gitano.
5. He did not want him to stay and was quite rude in his attempts to get the old man to leave, telling him to go to his relatives, etc.
6. He came back because he wanted to die where he had been born.
7. Carl Tiflin's old horse, the first one he had ever had.
8. Gitano said the horse was old and no good.
9. A shiny rapier.
10. They disappeared together over the mountains.

Quiz Time Section 4: "The Promise" (page 25)
1. Accept appropriate responses.
2. An imaginary army with trumpets and drums.
3. By rubbing its throat gently.
4. She made cottage cheese by putting clabbered milk into a cotton bag, then hanging it up to drain.
5. He put up the five dollars to pay for having Nellie bred, but Jody had to promise to earn the money by working for it all summer.
6. He had caught several different small animals and left them in his lunch pail, so when she went to clean the pail the animals were there.
7. He had to work to earn it by doing many chores.
8. Jody had many questions about how colts are born, and Billy Buck answered them.
9. Jody asked, "You won't let anything happen to the colt, will you?" Billy Buck was hurt, because he knew that Jody still held him responsible for the red pony's death.
10. He had to kill Nellie and take out the colt.

Quiz Time Section 5: "The Leader of the People" (page 30)
1. Accept appropriate responses.
2. Mice.
3. Her father, Jody's grandfather.
4. Because he talks a lot and retells the same stories.
5. An old man dressed in a black suit and tie, carrying a black slouch hat; white beard, white eyebrows, blue eyes; had "granite dignity," merry eyes, slow-moving; accept all accurate descriptions.
6. Named Mule-Pack because he packed mules.
7. They would eat their oxen and cattle.
8. The westward movement, moving west.
9. He was the leader of a wagon train.
10. He sees him as a hero, part of a race of giants no longer around, riding a huge white horse.

The Red Pony

Answer Key (cont.)

Objective Test and Essay (page 41)

Matching

1. F
2. G
3. I
4. L
5. H
6. C
7. K
8. D
9. J
10. B
11. E
12. A

True or False

1. False
2. True
3. False
4. False
5. True

Short Answer

1. Billy Buck made the hackamore.
2. Billy Buck taught him, talked to him, showed him.
3. The setting is the Salinas Valley during the early 1900's.
4. Carl Tiflin felt that Grandfather talked too much, he was boring, and he lived in the past.
5. Grandfather got to the ocean and thought he had gone as far as he could go.

Essay

Accept responses which include these or other appropriate answers: Jody hero-worships his grandfather, thinks he came from a line of giants which does not exist any longer, loves to listen to his stories. Jody asks him many questions about the old west. Jody follows Billy Buck around, listens to him, thinks he was always right until Billy makes a mistake about it not raining and the pony dies; Billy is his teacher around the ranch and with horses, and Jody asks him many questions about animals. Jody is a little afraid of his father, very shy with him, and is afraid to show feelings around him because his father does not show feelings. He is almost so shy with his father that he is afraid to talk to him.